The First World War

Contents

The war begins   2

The call to war   4

The battlegrounds   6

Trench life   8

Keeping spirits up   10

Weapons   12

Planes, tanks and submarines   14

Poison gas   16

Battlefield hospitals   18

The home front   20

Women and children in wartime   22

The end of the war   24

Peace and remembrance   26

Glossary   28

Index   29

War in the trenches and war at home   30

Written by Jillian Powell

Collins

The war begins

It was June 1914. **Archduke** Franz Ferdinand was next in line to the throne of Austria-Hungary. When he and his wife were visiting Bosnia, a gunman shot them dead. The gunman wanted Bosnia to join with Serbia, instead of being ruled by Austria-Hungary.

This photograph shows Archduke Franz Ferdinand and his wife minutes before they were shot.

The First World War lasted from 1914 to 1918. It killed around 23 million people and injured millions more.

Britain went to war with Germany on 4 August 1914, after Germany sent troops to invade France through Belgium, which was not at war.

Many men joined up to fight for Britain. The war was fought on land, in the air and at sea.

This map shows the countries in Europe which were fighting against each other by 1917. The countries coloured in yellow fought together against the countries coloured in red. The other countries shown were not part of the war.

Germany

Austria-Hungary

Serbia

The call to war

In the first few months after Britain went to war, more than 750,000 men joined the army. Many saw the war as a great adventure and joined up with friends from their towns, factories or football teams.

The new soldiers went to training camps for months of fitness and weapons training. All over Britain, people came out to watch them on parade before they were sent by special trains and troop ships to the battlegrounds.

Follow me!

YOUR COUNTRY NEEDS YOU

soldiers practising **bayonet** fighting

soldiers in Southampton marching to a troop ship

By 1916, more soldiers were needed because fewer men were **volunteering**, so the government passed a law to make all young and middle-aged men fight for Britain. Not all people agreed with this law, which was called conscription. Some men were punished for refusing to fight.

5

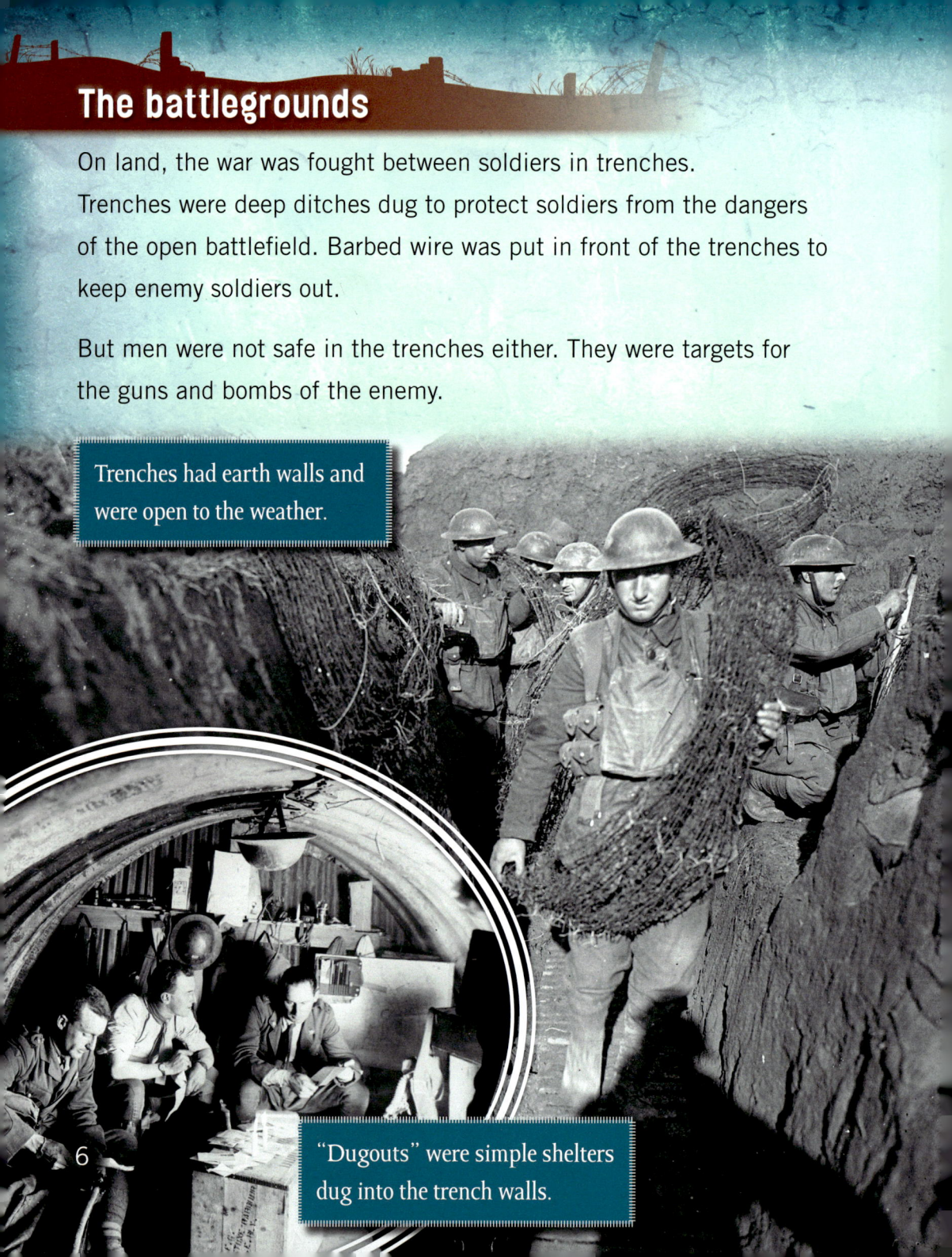

The battlegrounds

On land, the war was fought between soldiers in trenches. Trenches were deep ditches dug to protect soldiers from the dangers of the open battlefield. Barbed wire was put in front of the trenches to keep enemy soldiers out.

But men were not safe in the trenches either. They were targets for the guns and bombs of the enemy.

Trenches had earth walls and were open to the weather.

"Dugouts" were simple shelters dug into the trench walls.

To take land from the enemy, soldiers had to leave their trenches by climbing "over the top" and crossing the land between the trenches. They called this "No Man's Land". Once in the open, it was easier for the enemy to shoot at them or blow them up with **shells**.

Trench life

Life in the trenches was hard. There was constant danger and noise from shells and gunfire. Soldiers took turns to man the trenches for a few days at a time.

They slept in dugout shelters or on steps cut into the walls. They lived mostly on tinned food, like corned beef, and dry biscuits because it was hard to get and cook fresh food.

In winter it was often below freezing, and rain turned the land to mud and the trenches flooded. The men were sometimes up to their waists in water and had to live in wet clothes until they dried out.

Early in the war, many men in the trenches suffered from "trench foot", which made their feet red, swollen and painful. It was caused by wearing boots that stayed damp in the cold and mud. As the war went on, soldiers learnt to rub their feet with whale grease and change their socks to prevent trench foot.

Soldiers wade through mud in a trench.

A medical officer inspects soldiers' feet.

Keeping spirits up

When they were not in the trenches, the soldiers had time to rest behind the fighting lines. Some took up hobbies like drawing and woodcarving. They sang songs, played cards, wrote home and visited cafés. They looked forward to getting letters and parcels of food from their families. Sometimes the **Red Cross** also sent the soldiers extra supplies.

When the first Christmas of the war came, small groups of British and German soldiers stopped fighting and crossed to enemy trenches to swap gifts and play football. There were no orders telling soldiers to do this – the men just decided to do it themselves. But it was now clear the war wouldn't be a short one, and some army **generals** worried that this could weaken their soldiers' will to fight.

In this artist's picture of Christmas 1914, a German soldier approaches British lines with a small Christmas tree.

Weapons

Trench warfare led to new weapons and ways of fighting. From inside the trenches men fired shells from **mortars** and bullets from machine guns at their enemy. Behind the trench lines, **artillery** guns fired shells across large distances. Some shells were packed with explosives to destroy trenches and enemy guns, killing and injuring anyone in range. Other shells exploded and released deadly metal pieces called shrapnel. Soldiers wore steel helmets to protect their heads from shrapnel.

When soldiers reached an enemy trench on foot, they attacked with hand grenades, knives, clubs and bayonets.

These soldiers are firing a machine gun.

British soldiers and the **Allies** used so many shells and bullets that a special government department was set up to make sure that they had enough weapons and **ammunition** to keep fighting. New factories were opened and others were taken over to make guns, shells, planes and tanks.

men and women working in an ammunition factory in 1917

Planes, tanks and submarines

Planes were widely used by both sides in the war. In the early years of the war, pilots flew over enemy lines to map and photograph enemy trenches, weapons stores and gun positions. This meant guns on the ground could be aimed at enemy targets.

As the war went on, planes were also used to attack the enemy by firing machine guns and dropping bombs. Midair gunfights often broke out between Allied and German planes. Flying was still a very new skill, and was often very dangerous.

The British first began using tanks in 1916 to try to break through enemy defences. The tanks were covered in armour and had rolling tracks which could travel over broken ground, but they moved slowly and often broke down.

At sea, **submarines** attacked enemy ships, and British and German ships formed **blockades** to cut off important supplies to each other's countries.

Poison gas

Both sides looked for new weapons to win the war. The French and Germans had begun trying out gas as a weapon in the first year of the war.

By 1916, both sides were firing shells that released poison gas where they landed. When men breathed the gas in, it choked them, killing some and damaging the lungs of others. Gas masks were sent to protect the soldiers in the trenches.

This picture shows German troops in a poison gas cloud. The soldiers are wearing gas masks.

In 1917, the Germans began using mustard gas which soldiers feared because they could not see or smell it. It could make them sick hours after they had breathed it in, burning their skin, eyes, and lungs. It could kill soldiers several days or even weeks after contact with it, or make its victims go blind.

Soldiers rang bells or banged on tin pans to warn of gas attacks to give men time to put their masks on.

Battlefield hospitals

Millions of men were wounded during attacks. Hospitals were set up in tents and in empty houses or churches near to the trenches to give injured soldiers urgent treatment. Motor ambulances and wagons pulled by horses carried the wounded to the hospitals.

If men were fit to fight again after their treatment, they were sent back. But if they were too sick or wounded to carry on, they were sent home for more treatment.

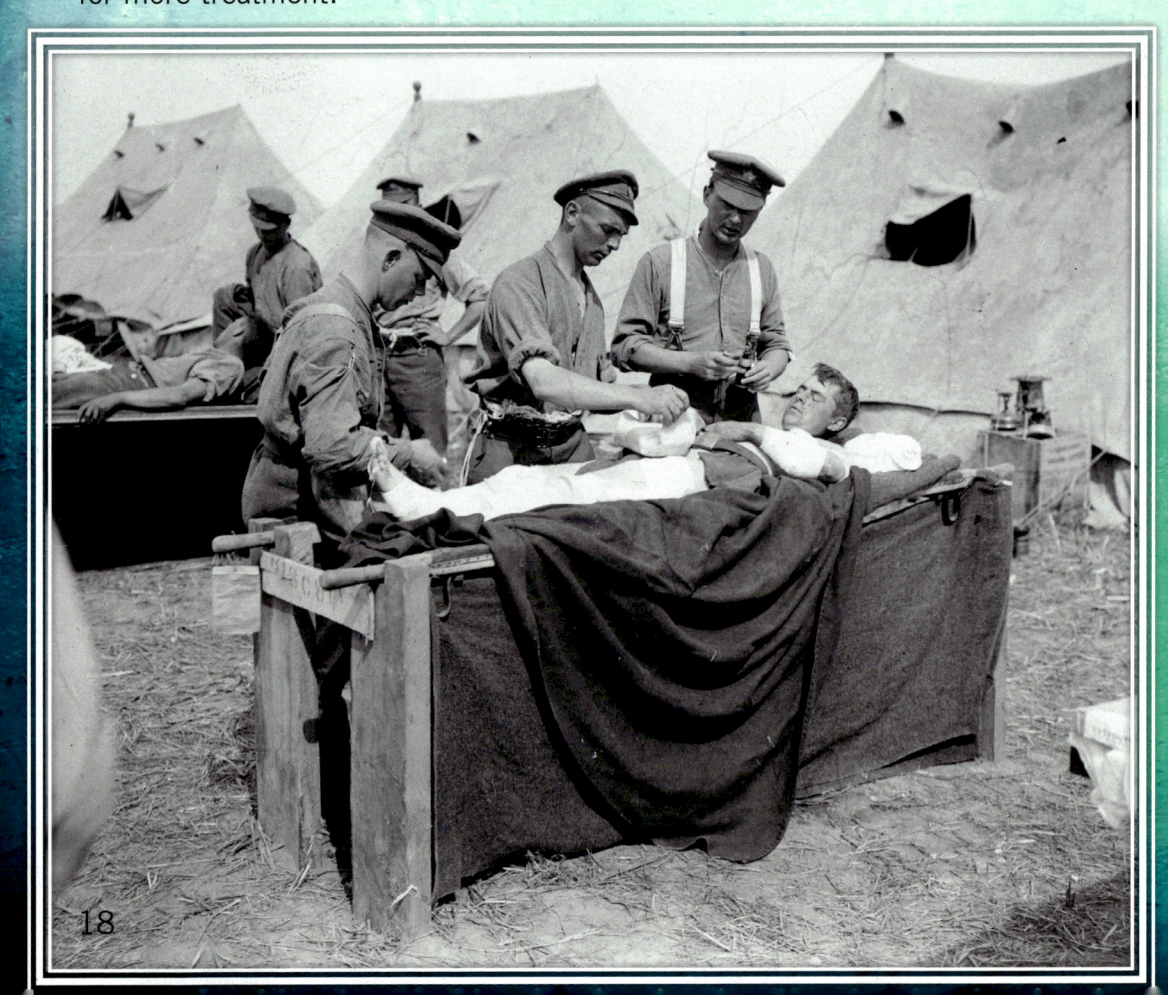

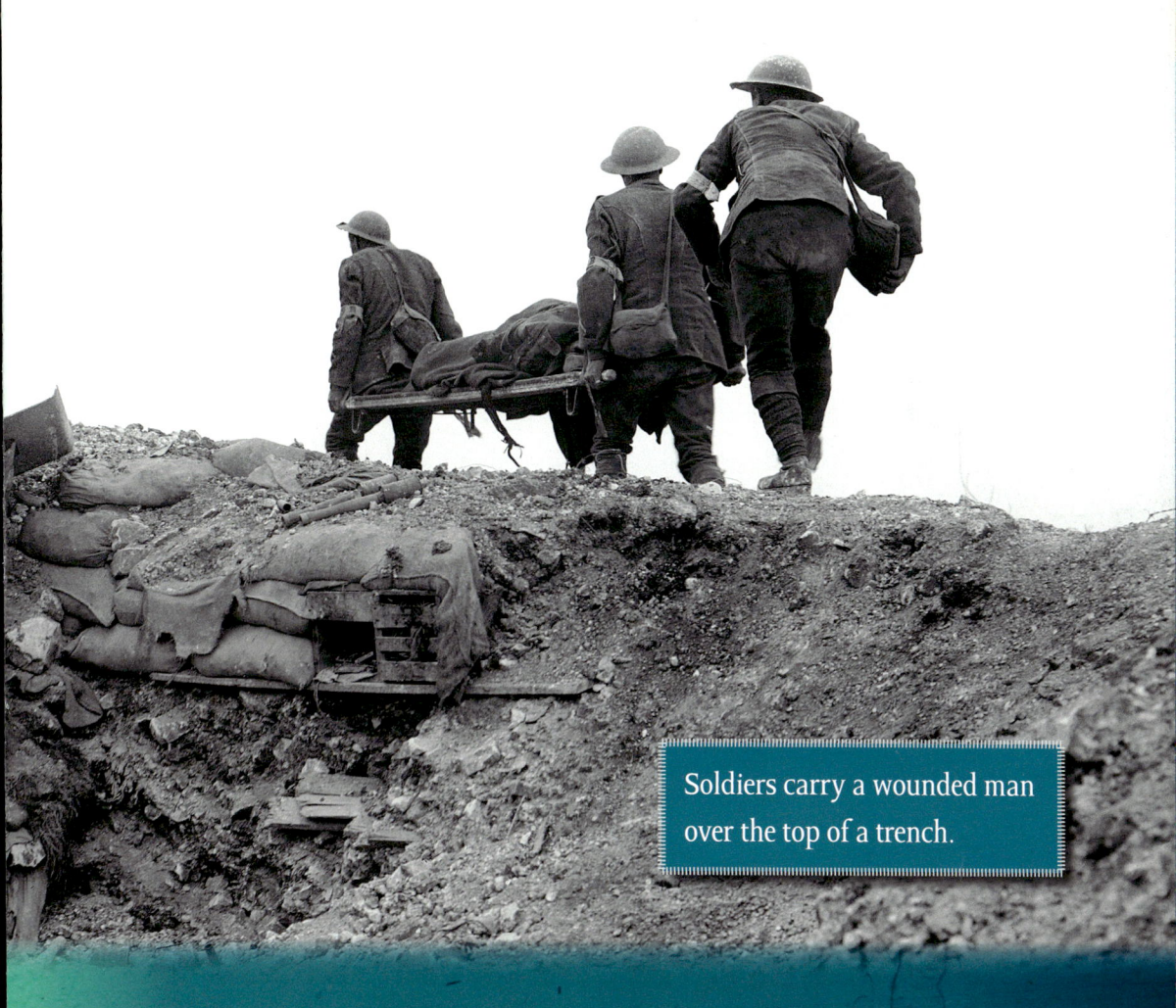

Soldiers carry a wounded man over the top of a trench.

Some men suffered from "shell shock". This was an illness that doctors only began to understand as the war went on. It could be brought on by shocking events, facing extreme danger for a long time, or the constant noise of guns and shelling. Soldiers with shell shock suffered extreme panic attacks and nightmares, which made them unable to fight.

The home front

At home, many people wanted to help the **war effort**. Some gave money or sold flags to raise funds to help the wounded. Others packed food parcels and knitted socks for the troops. People were keen to hear news of the war, but because there was no radio or television, they read newspapers and went to cinemas to find out what was happening.

These nurses are selling paper flags, worn like badges, to raise money for the war.

queueing for food in Reading in 1918

In Britain, the war took men and horses away from farms, and the German submarine blockade at sea made it harder for food from other countries to arrive by ship. To make sure that people got enough to eat, the government started rationing for the first time in 1918. Rationing meant that people had to use coupons to buy their share of sugar, meat, butter and cheese each week.

During the war, Germany used **airships** and bomber planes to attack Britain. Allied planes also bombed Germany. This was done to try to destroy weapons factories and to make ordinary people feel afraid.

Women and children in wartime

With many men away fighting, women took over jobs in transport, farming and factories that were usually done by men. Some women joined women's units in the armed forces. They looked after army trucks or did kitchen, office and telephone work. Others joined medical services like the Red Cross, as nurses.

working in an ammunition factory

working on a farm

fixing a car wheel

Children helped with the war effort too by driving milk carts, growing food on allotments and working in shops and on farms.

With their fathers away, many children also had to do more at home, such as looking after younger brothers and sisters while their mothers worked. Some older children wanted to do even more and lied about their age to join the army.

The First World War changed many children's lives forever when their fathers or elder brothers were killed.

Schoolboys dig up potatoes planted in their school playing field.

The end of the war

In 1916, the Allies began a "big push" to attack German trenches in the Somme valley in France to try to end the war. The Battle of the Somme lasted for four months and there were over a million **casualties**, but neither side won.

The Allies tried again to end the war with a huge battle at Ypres in Belgium, during the summer of 1917. Heavy rain turned the land to mud, and both sides were worn down again without a victory.

Allied soldiers cross a muddy battlefield.

But by then, things had begun to change. At sea, German submarines had been attacking Allied ships, even those carrying **civilians**. In 1915 they had sunk the passenger ship, the *Lusitania*. Hundreds of people, including many Americans, drowned. This was one of the events that led the USA to join the war against Germany in 1917.

In 1918, German forces began a series of huge attacks on the Allied troops in France and Belgium. They gained land but could not break through completely. The Allies fought to push the German army back, and were finally able to win the war.

American troops marching in France in 1918

Peace and remembrance

The war ended in 1918, at 11:00 a.m. on 11 November when the fighting stopped. This date is now called **Armistice** Day.

The countries that had been fighting met to make peace. People felt that it was important to remember the war and those who had died. In London, the **Cenotaph** was built and the tomb of the Unknown Warrior was placed in Westminster Abbey to remember the soldiers whose bodies had never been found.

The Cenotaph was unveiled on 11 November 1920.

an Armistice Day parade

People began selling poppies on Armistice Day each year to raise funds for wounded soldiers. Poppies became a symbol for fallen soldiers because red poppies grew on the battlefields in France and Belgium. Today, when we wear a poppy on 11 November, we remember them, and the men and women who have died in wars since.

Poppies like this one were sold in Britain from 1921.

27

Glossary

airships — aircraft like huge balloons with engines, that can be steered

Allies — the countries which fought together against Germany

ammunition — objects or explosive materials that are fired from weapons

Archduke — a high-ranking nobleman

armistice — an agreement to end a war

artillery — heavy guns like cannons

bayonet — a long knife that can be fixed to the end of a gun

blockade — using ships and submarines to stop ships using a port

casualties — soldiers injured, killed, missing or taken prisoner

Cenotaph — a memorial in London built to honour those killed in war

civilians — people who were not in the army, navy or air force

generals — army leaders

mortars — weapons that fire explosive ammunition

Red Cross — a charity that cares for people affected by wars and disasters

shells — bombs made by filling steel cases with explosive materials

submarines — sea craft that can travel both on and under water

volunteering — offering to do something without being made to

war effort — joining together to try and win the war

Index

ammunition   13

Armistice   26, 27

battlegrounds   4, 6

bombs   6, 14

Christmas   11

factories   4, 13, 21, 22

food   8, 10, 20, 21, 23

football   4, 11

gas   16, 17

guns   6, 12, 13, 14, 19

hospitals   18

mud   9, 24

mustard gas   17

No Man's Land   7

planes   14, 21

rationing   21

Red Cross   10, 22

sea   3, 15, 21, 25

shell shock   19

shells   7, 8, 12, 13, 16

ships   4, 15, 25

Somme   24

submarines   14, 15, 25

trenches   6, 7, 8, 9, 10, 11, 12, 14, 16, 18, 24

tanks   13, 14, 15

trench foot   9

weapons   4, 12, 13, 14, 16, 21

Ypres   24

War in the trenches

a dugout

wading through mud

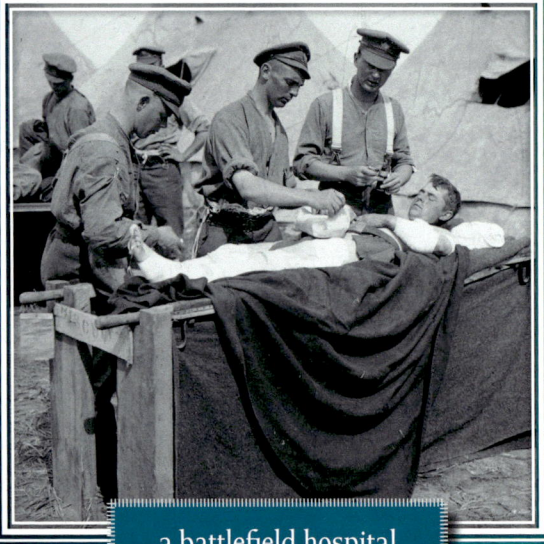

a battlefield hospital

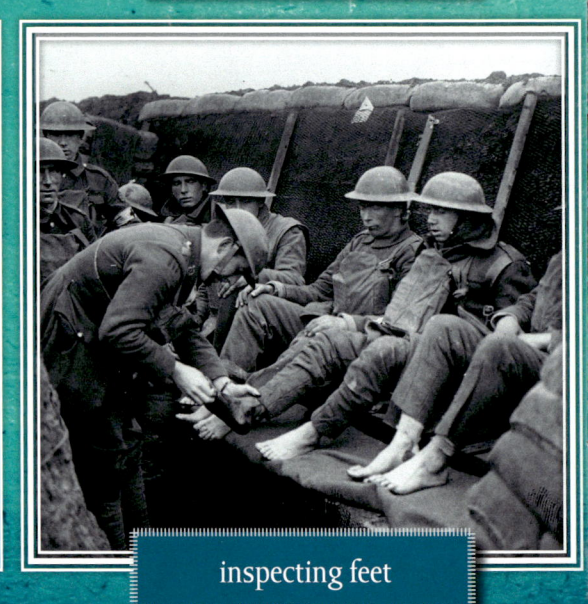

inspecting feet

War at home

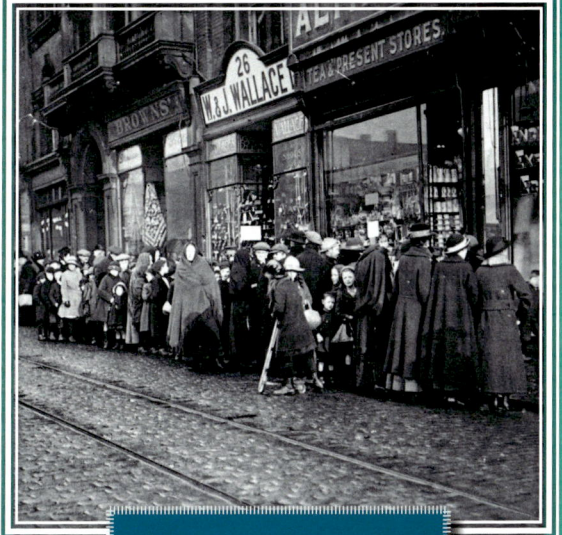

queueing for food

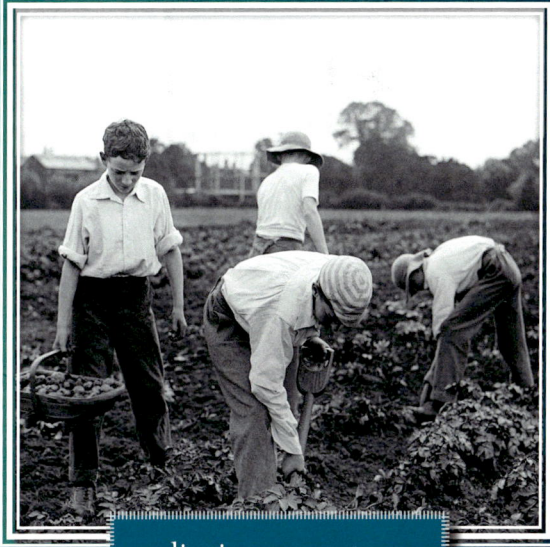

digging up potatoes

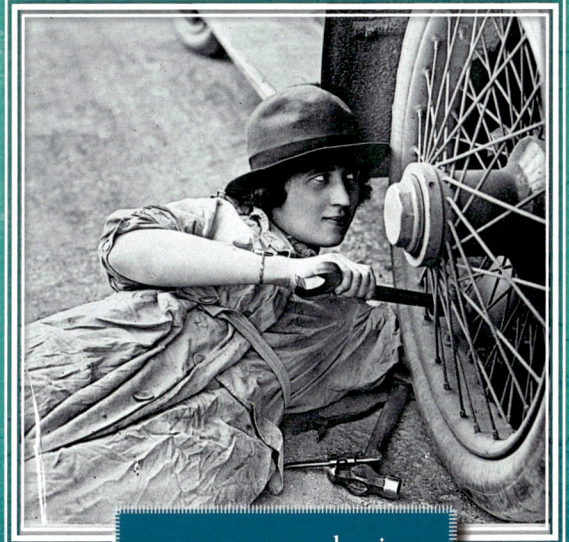

a woman mechanic

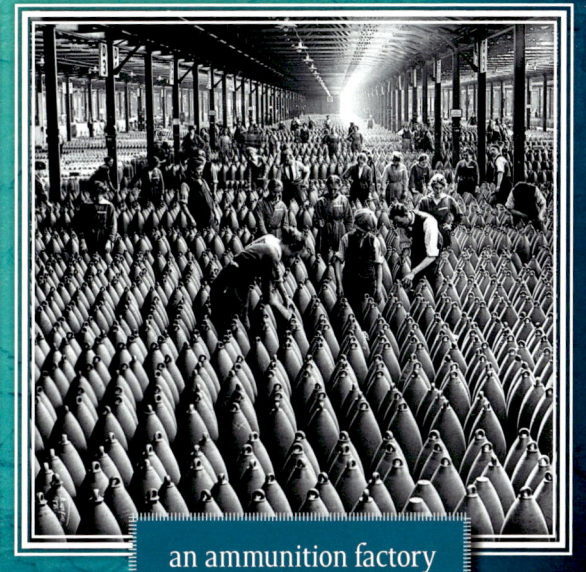

an ammunition factory

31

Ideas for reading

Written by Gillian Howell
Primary Literacy Consultant

Learning objectives: *(word reading objectives correspond with Lime band; all other objectives correspond with Sapphire band)* continue to apply phonic knowledge and skills as the route to decode words until automatic decoding has become embedded and reading is fluent; checking that the book makes sense to them, discussing their understanding and exploring the meaning of words in context; summarising the main ideas drawn from more than one paragraph, identifying key details that support the main ideas; provide reasoned justifications for their views

Curriculum links: History

Interest words: adventure, soldiers, weapons, government, conscription, biscuits, swollen, shrapnel, armour, ambulances, rationing, civilians, Cenotaph

Word count: 1,851

Resources: whiteboard, pens, paper

Getting started

- Ask the children to say what they already know about the First World War and note their responses on the whiteboard. Read the title together and look at the front cover. Ask the children what the photograph on the cover shows and what impression the photograph gives them. Who are the people in the picture?

- Ask the children to read the contents page aloud. If children struggle with any of the words, e.g. *remembrance*, remind them to break longer words into manageable chunks. Remind them to use their phonic knowledge and contextual clues when they come across new words.

- Point out the word *Archduke* on p2. Ask the children to say why it is written in bold print and turn to the glossary. Remind them to use the glossary to help them understand new terms in the text.

Reading and responding

- Ask the children to read the text aloud but in a quiet voice. Listen to the children as they read and prompt as necessary, e.g. give them the soft *g* sound in *danger* if they are struggling to read it.